World Regional Maps Coloring Book

Maps of World Regions, Continents, World Projections, USA and Canada

Blank, Outline and Detailed Maps for Coloring, Home School, Marketing and Education

Illustrations by J. Bruce Jones

www.BruceJonesPublishing.com

Dear Reader,

Thank you for buying World Regional Maps Coloring Book. I hope you have fun with it and it proves useful.

I enjoy receiving comments and suggestions from readers. Your ideas are always very helpful. I also love to hear how you are using our books. Are you just coloring for fun or using it to teach students in a classroom or at home? And is there additional information that you would have liked to find in this book - or in the next one?

So let me know - the good and the bad - and I will try to make even better books!

Thank you and keep coloring

Bruce
bruce@bjdesign.com

World Regional Maps Coloring Book
Maps fo World Regions, Continents, World Projections, USA and Canada
Blank, Outline and Detailed Maps for Coloring, Home School, Marketing and Education
Concept, creating, editing and illustrations by J. Bruce Jones

J. Bruce Jones
661 Washington Street
Norwood, MA 02062
781-255-7171
www.freeusandworldmaps.com
www.brucejonespublishing.com

World Regional Maps Coloring Book

World Map — Mercator Projection

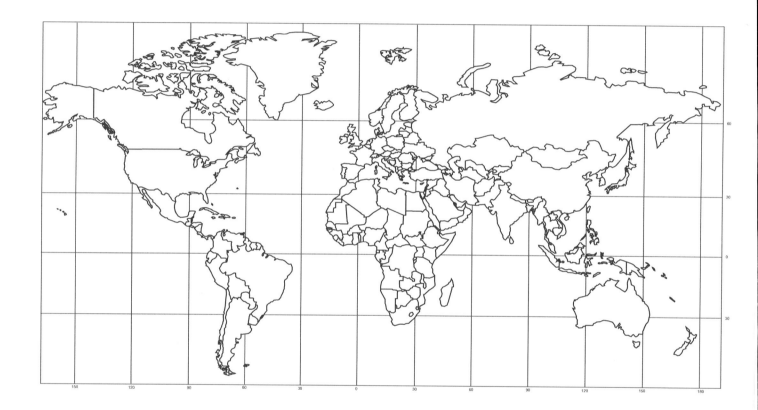

World Map — Mercator Projection

World Map — Mercator Projection

World Map — Robinson Projection

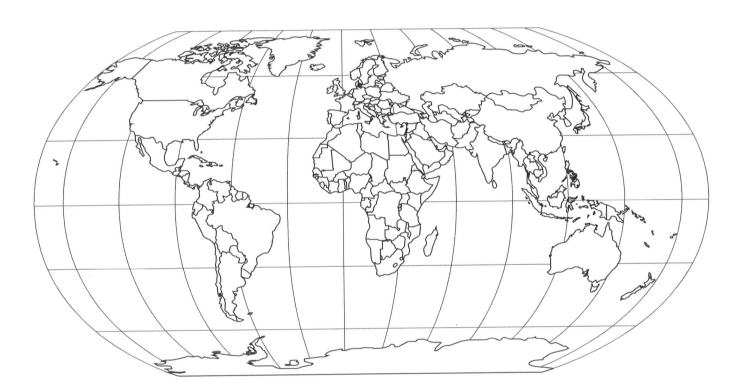

World Map — Robinson Projection

World Map — Robinson Projection

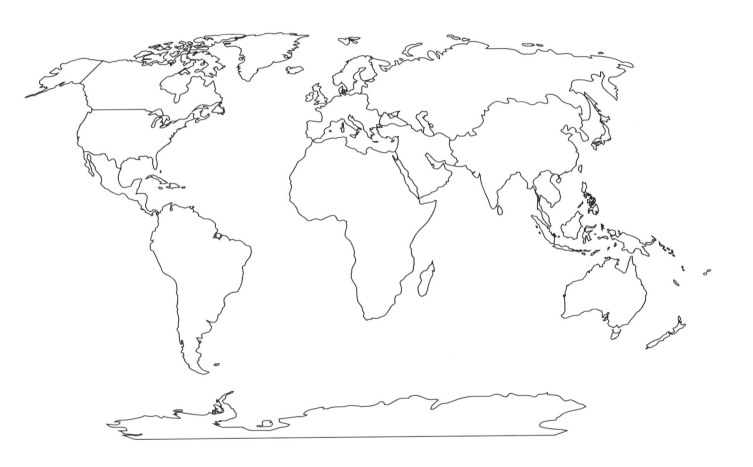

Europe Global Projection

North America Global Projection

Africa

Algiers
Tunis
TUNISIA
Casablanca Rabat Oran Constantine
MOROCCO
Mediterranean Sea
Marrakech Bechar
Tripoli
Banghazi Alexandria
Cairo
El Aaiun
WESTERN
SAHARA
ALGERIA
LIBYA
EGYPT
Al Jawf
Aswan
Red Sea
MAURITANIA MALI
NIGER
Faya-Largeau
SUDAN
Port Sudan
ERITREA
Nouakchott
Tamanrasset
Khartoum
Asmara
Dakar Nema
Lombouctou
Agadez
CHAD
Al Fashir
DJIBOUTI
Banjul SENEGAL
Bamako
Niamey
Zinder
Djibouti
THE
GAMBIA
Bissau
GUINEA
BISSAU
BURKINA
Kano Maiduguri N' Djamena
Berbera
Conakry
Ouagadougou
BENIN
NIGERIA
SOUTHERN
SUDAN
Addis
Ababa
Freetown
GUINEA
COTE
DTVOIRE
TOGO
Abuja
Waw
ETHIOPIA
SIERRA
LEONE
Monrovia
GHANA
Abidjan
Porto-Novo
Lagos
Loma
Accra
CENTRAL
AFRICAN
REPUBLIC
Juba
LIBERIA
CAMEROON
Bangui
Malabo
Yaounde
UGANDA
KENYA
SOMALIA
Mogadishu
EQUATORIAL
GUINEA
REP. OF
THE
CONGO
Kisangani
Kampala
Libreville
DEMOCRATIC
REPUBLIC
OF THE CONGO
(ZAIRE)
Kigali
*Lake
Victoria*
Nairobi
Indian
GABON
RWANDA
BURUNDI
Bujumbura
Mombasa
South
Brazzaville
Kalemie
*Lake
Tanganyika*
Zanzibar
Ocean
Pointe-Noire
Kinshasa
Kananga
TANZANIA
Dar es Salaam
Atlantic
ANGOLA
Luanda
Malanje
Mbeya
*Lake
Nyasa*
Ocean
Lobito
ANGOLA
MALAWI
Ndola
Lilongwe
Nacala
Namibe
Menongue
ZAMBIA
Lusaka
MADAGASCAR
Antananarivo
NAMIBIA
Harare
ZIMBABWE
Bulawayo
MOZAMBIQUE
Beira
Toliara
Windhoek
BOTSWANA
SOUTH AFRICA
Walvis Bay
Gaborone
Pretoria
Johannesburg
Maputo
SWAZILAND
Luderitz
Maseru
Mbabane
Indian
LESOTHO
Durban
SOUTH
AFRICA
Ocean
Cape Town
Port Elizabeth

0   500   1000 Nautical Miles

Africa

MOROCCO

TUNISIA

ALGERIA

LIBYA

EGYPT

WESTERN
SAHARA

MAURITANIA

MALI

NIGER

CHAD

SUDAN

ERITREA

SENEGAL

THE
GAMBIA

DJIBOUTI

GUINEA
BISSAU

BURKINA

GUINEA

NIGERIA

BENIN

TOGO

COTE
DTVOIRE

GHANA

SIERRA
LEONE

LIBERIA

CAMEROON

CENTRAL
AFRICAN
REPUBLIC

SOUTHERN
SUDAN

ETHIOPIA

SOMALIA

EQUATORIAL
GUINEA

REP. OF
THE
CONGO

UGANDA

KENYA

GABON

DEMOCRATIC
REPUBLIC
OF THE CONGO
(ZAIRE)

RWANDA

BURUNDI

Lake
Victoria

Indian

South

ANGOLA

Lake
Tanganyika

Zanzibar

Ocean

Atlantic

TANZANIA

Ocean

MALAWI

Lake
Nyasa

ANGOLA

ZAMBIA

MOZAMBIQUE

MADAGASCAR

ZIMBABWE

NAMIBIA

BOTSWANA

SOUTH AFRICA
Walvis Bay

SWAZILAND

Indian

0   500   1000 Nautical Miles

LESOTHO

SOUTH
AFRICA

Ocean

Africa

14

Africa

Antarctic Region

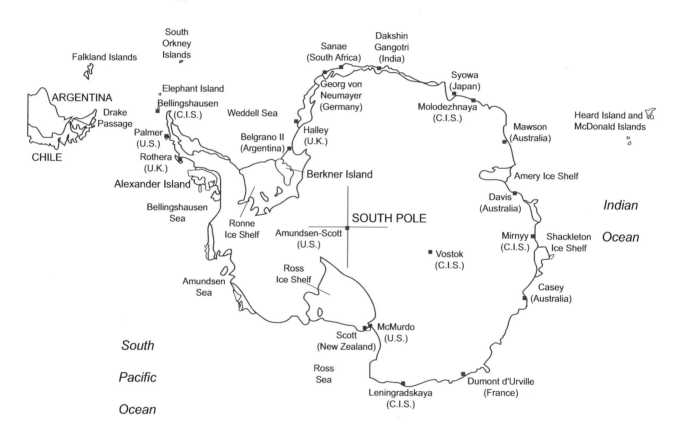

South

Atlantic

Ocean

South Georgia and the
South Sandwich Islands

South
Orkney
Islands

Sanae
(South Africa)

Dakshin
Gangotri
(India)

Falkland Islands

Syowa
(Japan)

ARGENTINA

Elephant Island

Bellingshausen
(C.I.S.)

Georg von
Neumayer
(Germany)

Molodezhnaya
(C.I.S.)

Heard Island and
McDonald Islands

Drake
Passage

Weddell Sea

Mawson
(Australia)

Palmer
(U.S.)

Halley
(U.K.)

CHILE

Belgrano II
(Argentina)

Rothera
(U.K.)

Amery Ice Shelf

Alexander Island

Berkner Island

Davis
(Australia)

Indian

Bellingshausen
Sea

SOUTH POLE

Ocean

Ronne
Ice Shelf

Mirnyy
(C.I.S.)

Shackleton
Ice Shelf

Amundsen-Scott
(U.S.)

Vostok
(C.I.S.)

Ross
Ice Shelf

Amundsen
Sea

Casey
(Australia)

South

McMurdo
(U.S.)

Scott
(New Zealand)

Pacific

Ross
Sea

Dumont d'Urville
(France)

Ocean

Leningradskaya
(C.I.S.)

■ Selected year-round research station

0   500   1000 Nautical Miles

NEW
ZEALAND

AUSTRALIA

Antarctic Region

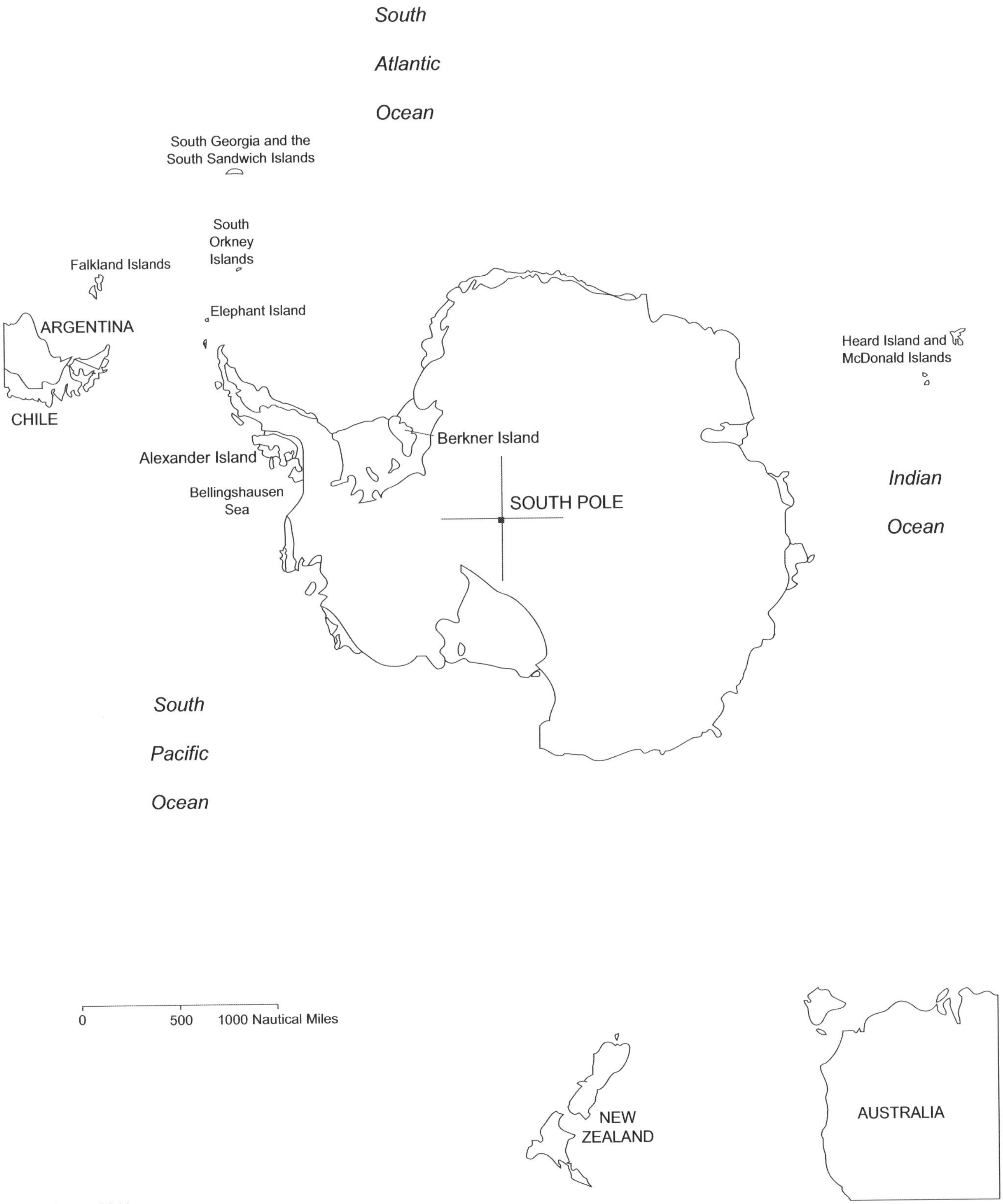

South

Atlantic

Ocean

South Georgia and the
South Sandwich Islands

South
Orkney
Islands

Falkland Islands

ARGENTINA

Elephant Island

CHILE

Heard Island and
McDonald Islands

Alexander Island

Berkner Island

Bellingshausen
Sea

SOUTH POLE

Indian

Ocean

South

Pacific

Ocean

0   500   1000 Nautical Miles

NEW
ZEALAND

AUSTRALIA

Antarctic Region

Australia, Oceania

CHINA

Okinawa

Taipei

TAIWAN

Hong Kong
Macau

South

China

Sea

PHILIPPINES

Manila

Philippine Sea

MALAYSIA
BRUNEI

Pacific Ocean

Wewak

New Ireland

INDONESIA

PAPUA
NEW GUINEA

New
Britain

Bougainville

SOLOMON
ISLANDS

Honiara

Arafura Sea

Port
Moresby

Timor Sea

Darwin

Coral Sea

VANUATU

FIJI

Port-Vila

Suva

Indian Ocean

Dampier

Cairns

Great
Barrier
Reef

New
Caledonia

Noumea

Alice Springs

Rockhampton

AUSTRALIA

Perth

Brisbane

Norfolk Island

Kingston

Broken Hill

Whyalla

Sydney

Canberra

Great Australian
Bight

North
Island

Melbourne

Auckland

Tasman Sea

NEW
ZEALAND

Indian Ocean

Launceston

Tasmania

Greymouth

Wellington

Christchurch

South
Island

0   500 Nautical Miles

Stewart Island

Australia, Oceania

CHINA

Okinawa

TAIWAN

Hong Kong
Macau

South

China

Sea

PHILIPPINES

Philippine Sea

Pacific Ocean

MALAYSIA
BRUNEI

New Ireland

INDONESIA

PAPUA
NEW GUINEA

New
Britain

Bougainville

SOLOMON
ISLANDS

Arafura Sea

Timor Sea

Indian Ocean

Great
Barrier
Reef

Coral Sea

VANUATU

FIJI

New
Caledonia

AUSTRALIA

Norfolk Island

Tasman Sea

NEW
ZEALAND

North
Island

Indian Ocean

Tasmania

South
Island

Stewart Island

0   500 Nautical Miles

Australia, Oceania

Australia

Indian Ocean

Darwin

Gulf of Carpantaria

Coral Sea

Katherine

NORTHERN TERRITORY

Cairns

Derby

Broome

Mount Isa

Mackay

WESTERN AUSTRALIA

Alice Springs

QUEENSLAND

Carnarvon

Charleville

Meekatharra

Brisbane

SOUTH AUSTRALIA

Leigh Creek

Bourke

Kalgoorlie

Ceduna

Broken Hill

Port Macquarie

Perth

Fremantle

Port Pine

NEW SOUTH WALES

Adeliade

Esperance

Canberra

Sydney

Great Australian Bight

VICTORIA

Melbourne

Bairnsdale

Tasman Sea

0   500 Kilometers

TASMANIA

0   500 Miles

Hobart

Indian Ocean

Australia

23

Southeast Asia

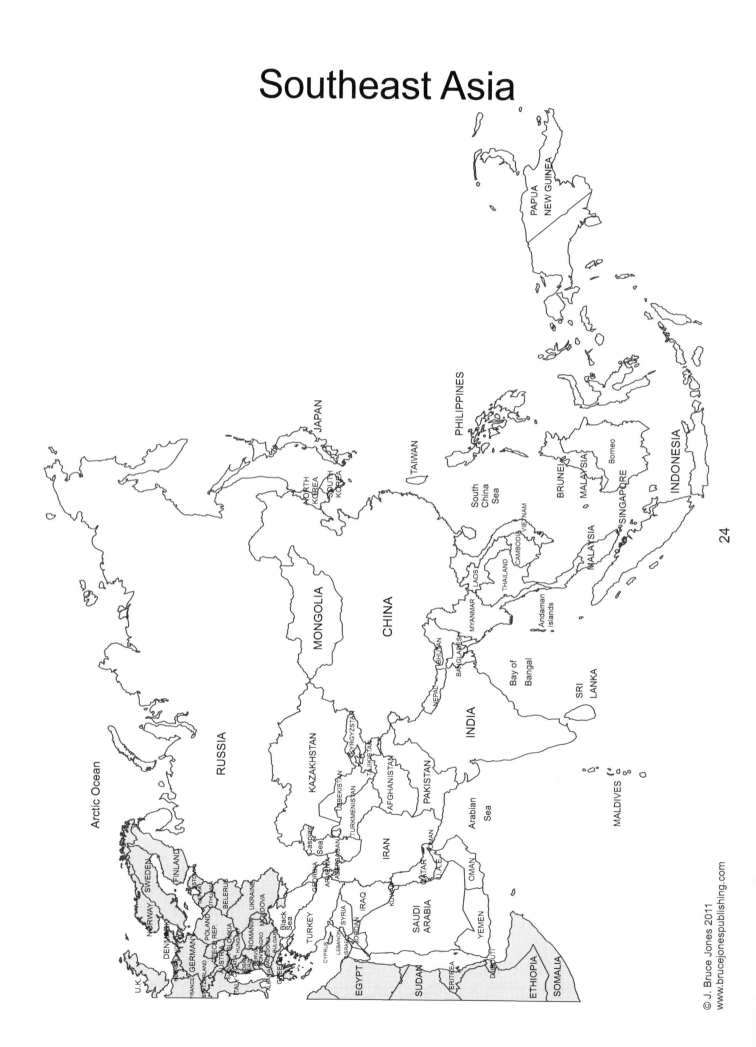

Southeast Asia

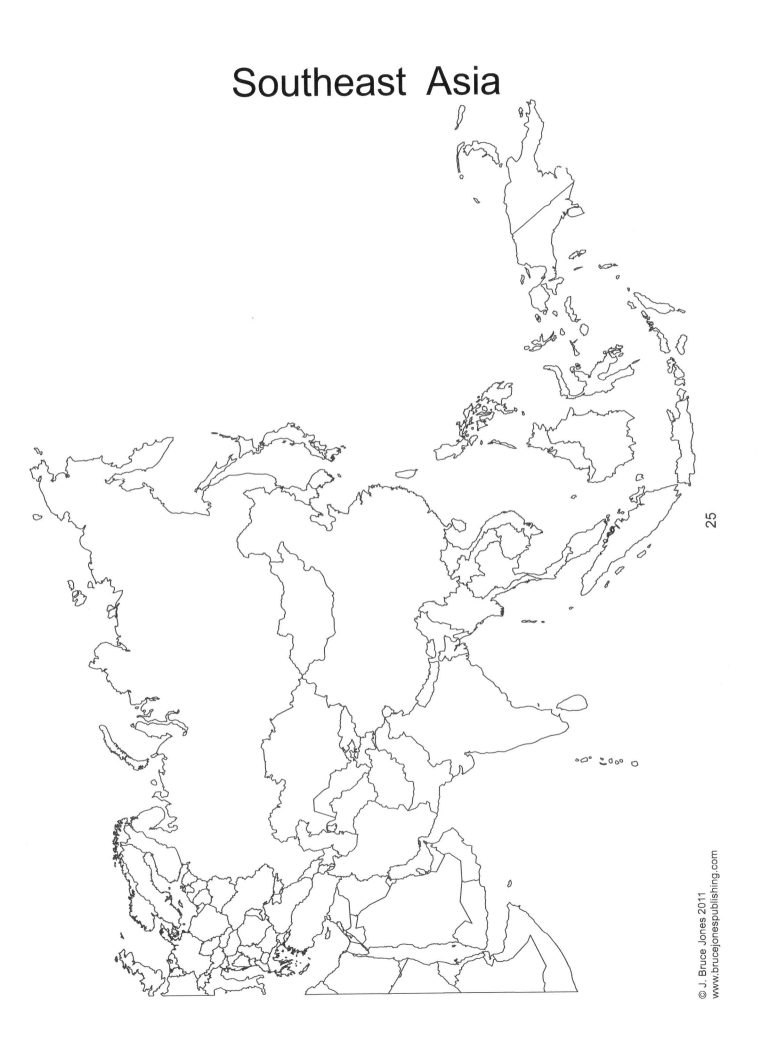

Asia

© J. Bruce Jones 2011
www.brucejonespublishing.com

26

Asia

Arctic Ocean

Svalbard

U.K

DENMARK
NORWAY
SWEDEN
GERMANY
ESTONIA   FINLAND
POLAND
LATVIA
LITHUANIA

Novaya Zemlya

Severnaya Zemlya

New Siberian Islands

U.S.

Wrangel Island

Bering Sea

North Pacific Ocean

RUSSIA

Sea of Okhotsk

ROM.

Black Sea

Lake Baikal

TURKEY

Caspian Sea
Aral Sea

Lake Balkhash

MONGOLIA

NORTH KOREA

IRAQ

SOUTH KOREA

JAPAN

KUWAIT
IRAN
AFGHANISTAN

East

CHINA

China

QATAR
OMAN
PAKISTAN

Sea

SAUDI ARABIA

NEPAL
BHUTAN

TAIWAN

BANGLADESH

Hong Kong

Philippine

INDIA

Luzon

Sea

Arabian

BURMA

LAOS

Hainan Dao

Sea

Bay of

THAILAND

VIETNAM

PHILIPPINES

Andaman Islands

CAMBODIA

South China Sea

Bangal

SRI LANKA

Nicobar Islands

BRUNEI

MALDIVES

MALAYSIA
MALAYSIA

INDONESIA

Sumatra   SINGAPORE

INDONESIA

0   500   1000 Nautical Miles

Asia

Asia

Russia

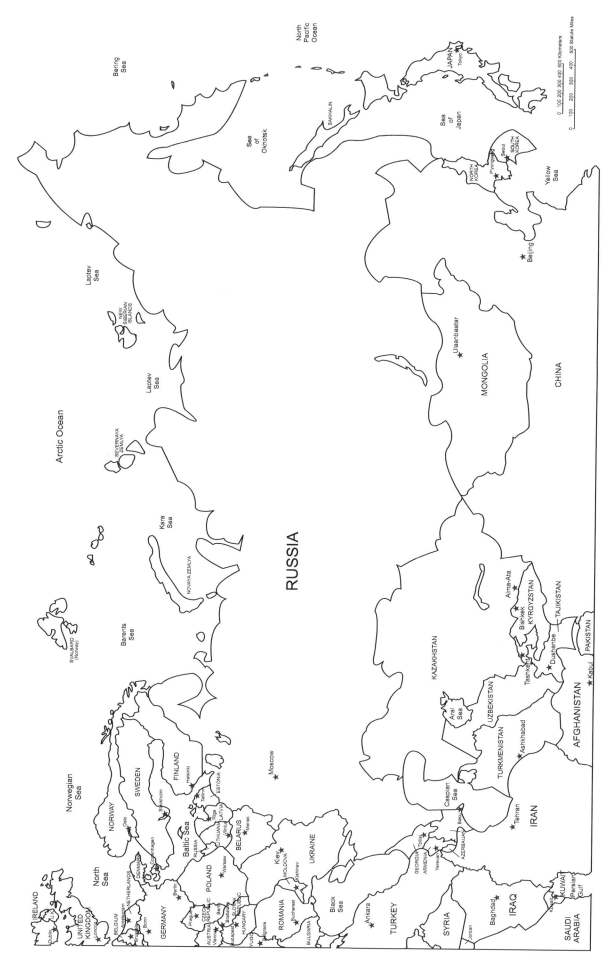

30

Russia

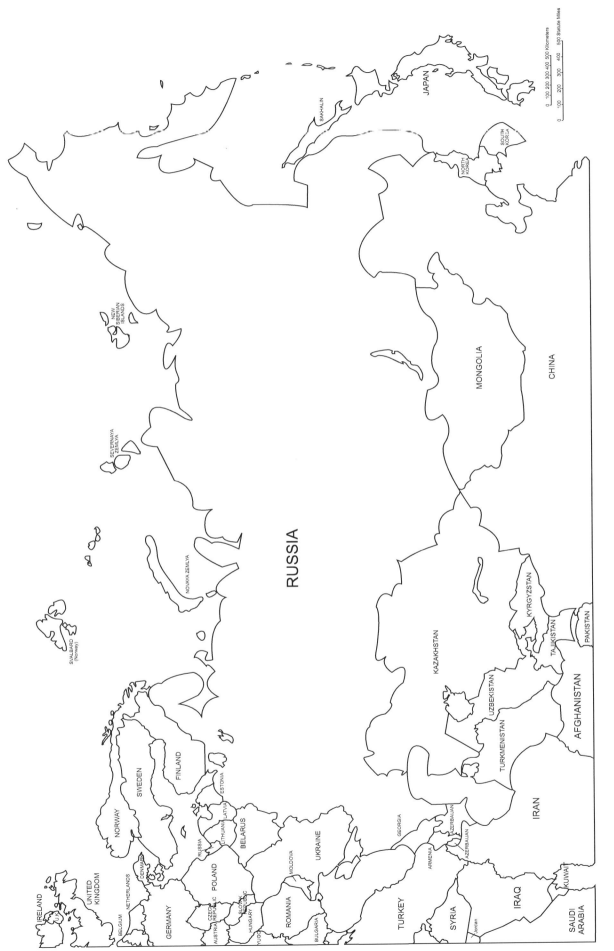

IRELAND

UNITED
KINGDOM

NORWAY

SWEDEN

FINLAND

SVALBARD
(Norway)

NOVAYA ZEMLYA

SEVERNAYA
ZEMLYA

NEW
SIBERIAN
ISLANDS

RUSSIA

BELGIUM

NETHERLANDS

GERMANY

DENMARK

CZECH
REPUBLIC

AUSTRIA

SLOVAK
REPUBLIC

HUNGARY

YUGO

POLAND

ROMANIA

BULGARIA

RUSSIA

LITHUANIA

LATVIA

ESTONIA

BELARUS

MOLDOVA

UKRAINE

GEORGIA

ARMENIA

AZERBAIJAN

AZERBAIJAN

TURKEY

SYRIA

IRAQ

Jordan

KUWAIT

SAUDI
ARABIA

IRAN

KAZAKHSTAN

UZBEKISTAN

TURKMENISTAN

KYRGYZSTAN

TAJIKISTAN

PAKISTAN

AFGHANISTAN

MONGOLIA

CHINA

JAPAN

SAKHALIN

NORTH
KOREA

SOUTH
KOREA

0 100 200 300 400 500 Kilometers

0   100   200   300   400   500 Statute Miles

31

Russia

Central America and the Caribbean

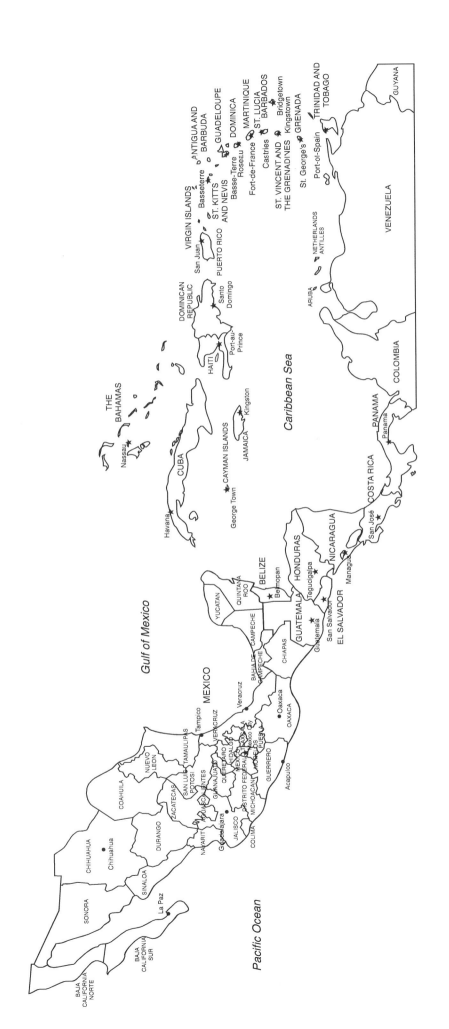

Central America and the Caribbean

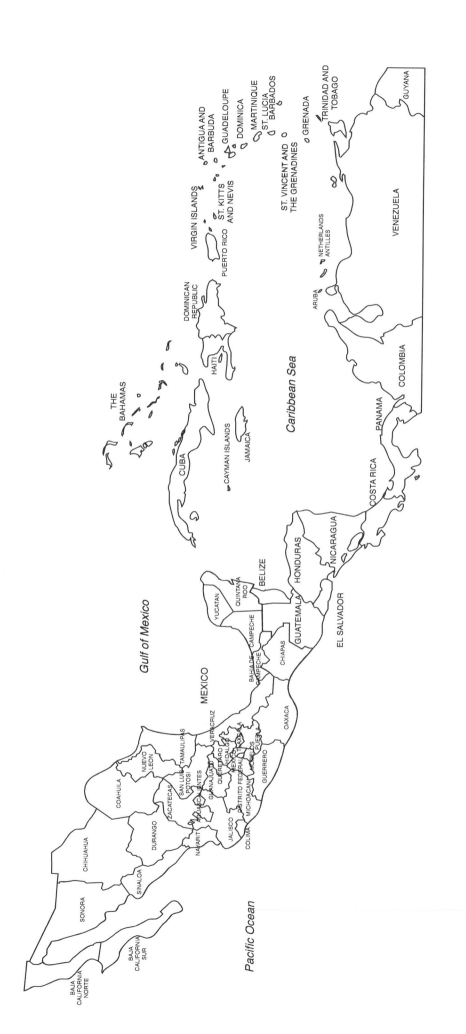

34

Central America

Central America

Atlantic Ocean

ARIZONA NEW MEXICO

TEXAS

ARKANSAS

MISSISSIPPI ALABAMA GEORGIA

LOUISIANA

FLORDIA

THE
BAHAMAS

Gulf of Mexico

MEXICO

CUBA

DOMINICAN
REPUBLIC

HAITI

Pacific Ocean

CAYMAN ISLANDS

JAMAICA

BELIZE

Caribbean Sea

GUATEMALA

HONDURAS

EL SALVADOR NICARAGUA

COSTA RICA PANAMA

COLOMBIA

Central America

Europe

Europe

ICELAND

FAROE
ISLANDS

SHETLAND
ISLANDS

ORKNEY
ISLANDS

HERBRIDES

North
Atlantic
Ocean

NORWAY

SWEDEN

FINLAND

RUSSIA

ESTONIA

LATVIA

LITHUANIA

DENMARK

RUSSIA

BELARUS

UNITED

KINGDOM

IRELAND

NETHERLANDS

BELGIUM

GERMANY

POLAND

UKRAINE

LUX.

CZECH REPUBLIC

SLOVAKIA

MOLDOVA

AUSTRIA

HUNGARY

ROMANIA

FRANCE

LIECHTENSTEIN

SWITZERLAND

SLOVENIA

CROATIA

BOSNIA AND
HERZEGOVINA

SERBIA

BULGARIA

MONACO

ITALY

MONTENEGRO

KOSOVO

ANDORRA

Corsica
FRANCE

F.Y.R.O.M

ALB.

TURKEY

PORTUGAL

Sardinia
ITALY

GREECE

SPAIN

BALEARIC
ISLANDS

Rhodes

Crete

MALTA

MOROCCO

ALGERIA

TUNISIA

0		300 Kilometers
0		300 Miles

Europe

Europe

42

Europe to the Ural Mountains

RUSSIA

RUSSIA

KAZAKHSTAN

UZBEKISTAN

TURKMENISTAN

IRAN

Tehran

Caspian Sea

Baku

AZERBAIJAN

ARMENIA

Yerevan

GEORGIA

Tbilisi

IRAQ

Baghdad

SYRIA

Damascus

Beirut

LEBANON

CYPRUS

Nicosia

TURKEY

Ankara

Black Sea

Moscow

Murmansk

Barents Sea

White Sea

Norwegian Sea

North Sea

FINLAND

Helsinki

Lake Ladoga

St. Petersburg

Tallinn

ESTONIA

LATVIA

Riga

Gulf of Finland

Gulf of Bothnia

SWEDEN

NORWAY

Oslo

Stavanger

Goteborg

Stockholm

Gotland

Oland

Bornholm

Baltic Sea

Kaliningrad

LITHUANIA

Vilnius

RUSSIA

Minsk

BELARUS

Brest

UKRAINE

Kiev

Rvne

MOLDOVA

Chisinau

Odesa

ROMANIA

Bucharest

BULGARIA

Sofia

SERBIA

Belgrade

Pristina

KOSOVO

F.Y.R.O.M.

Skopje

GREECE

Athens

ALB.

Tirana

MONTENEGRO

Podgorica

Ionian Sea

BOSNIA HERZEGOVINA

Sarajevo

CROATIA

Zagreb

SLOVENIA

Ljubljana

HUNGARY

Budapest

SLOVAKIA

Bratislava

Vienna

AUSTRIA

Warsaw

Krakow

POLAND

Gdansk

Prague

CZECH REPUBLIC

Berlin

Leipzig

Bremen

Hamburg

Munich

GERMANY

DENMARK

Copenhagen

NETHERLANDS

Amsterdam

Brussels

BELGIUM

LUX.

Luxembourg

Strasbourg

Bern

SWITZ.

Geneva

Lyon

FRANCE

Paris

Bordeaux

Bay of Biscay

ITALY

Venice

Genoa

Rome

Naples

Palermo

Sicily

Tyrrhenian Sea

Ligurian Sea

Corsica

FRANCE

Sardinia

ITALY

Cagliari

MONACO

Marseille

ANDORRA

V ella

Barcelona

Balearic Sea

BALEARIC ISLANDS

SPAIN

Madrid

Valencia

Sevilla

Gibraltar

Alboran Sea

PORTUGAL

Lisbon

Porto

Celtic Sea

IRELAND

Dublin

Belfast

UNITED KINGDOM

London

Leeds

Edinburgh

Irish Sea

English Channel

HERBRIDES

ORKNEY ISLANDS

SHETLAND ISLANDS

FAROE ISLANDS

ICELAND

Reykjavik

Atlantic Ocean

Mediterranean Sea

Valletta

MALTA

Tunis

TUNISIA

Algiers

ALGERIA

Rabat

MOROCCO

LIBYA

Crete

Bucharest

SERBIA

Lyon

300 Miles
300 Kilometers
0
0

43

Europe to the Ural Mountains

300 Kilometers

300 Miles

ICELAND

FAROE ISLANDS

SHETLAND ISLANDS

ORKNEY ISLANDS

HERBRIDES

NORTHERN IRELAND

IRELAND

UNITED KINGDOM

NORWAY

SWEDEN

FINLAND

RUSSIA

RUSSIA

DENMARK

NETHERLANDS

BELGIUM

LUX.

ESTONIA

LATVIA

LITHUANIA

RUSSIA

Gotland

BELARUS

POLAND

UKRAINE

FRANCE

SWITZ.

LIECH.

CZECH REPUBLIC

SLOVAKIA

AUSTRIA

HUNGARY

SLOVENIA

CROATIA

MOLDOVA

ROMANIA

BOSNIA AND HERZEGOVINA

MONTENEGRO

SERBIA

KOSOVO

BULGARIA

F.Y.R.O.M.

ALB.

GREECE

MONACO

ITALY

Corsica
FRANCE

Sardinia
ITALY

ANDORRA

BALEARIC ISLANDS

SPAIN

PORTUGAL

MOROCCO

ALGERIA

TUNISIA

MALTA

LIBYA

Crete

KAZAKHSTAN

UZBEKISTAN

TURKMENISTAN

GEORGIA

AZERBAIJAN

ARMENIA

IRAN

TURKEY

IRAQ

SYRIA

LEBANON

CYPRUS

44

Europe to the Ural Mountains

45

Middle East

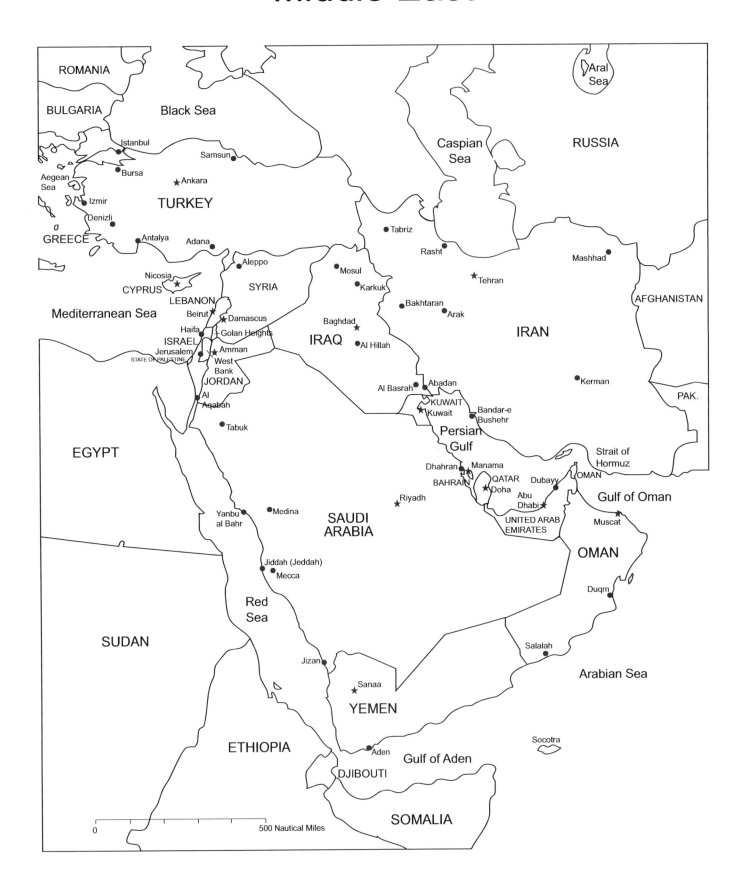

Middle East

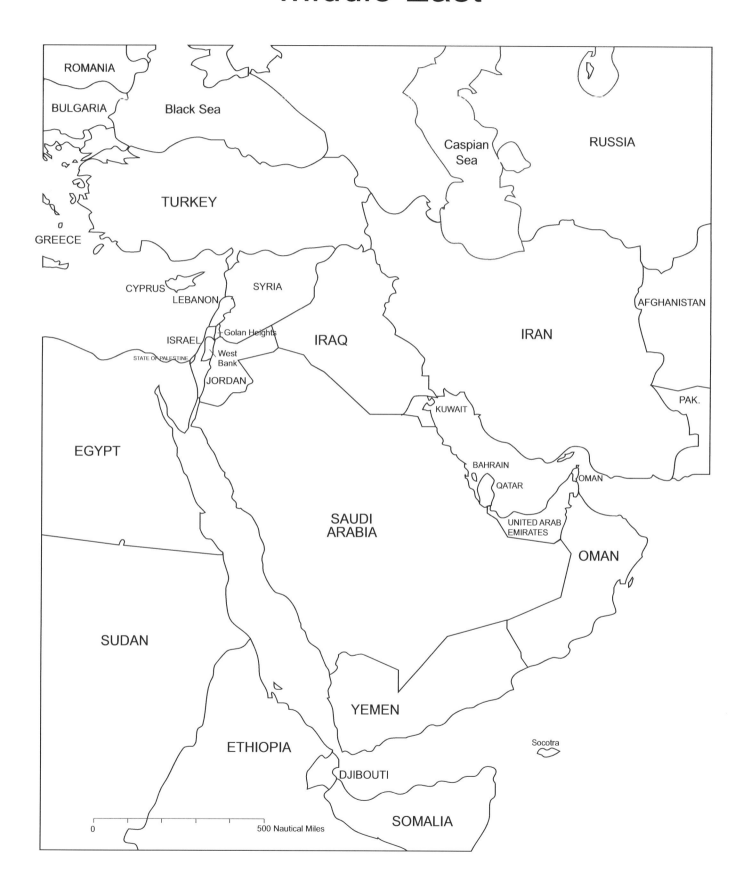

ROMANIA

BULGARIA

Black Sea

Caspian Sea

RUSSIA

TURKEY

GREECE

CYPRUS

SYRIA

LEBANON

AFGHANISTAN

ISRAEL

Golan Heights

IRAQ

IRAN

STATE OF PALESTINE

West Bank

JORDAN

KUWAIT

PAK.

EGYPT

BAHRAIN

QATAR

OMAN

UNITED ARAB EMIRATES

SAUDI ARABIA

OMAN

SUDAN

YEMEN

ETHIOPIA

Socotra

DJIBOUTI

0   500 Nautical Miles

SOMALIA

47

Middle East

48

Middle East

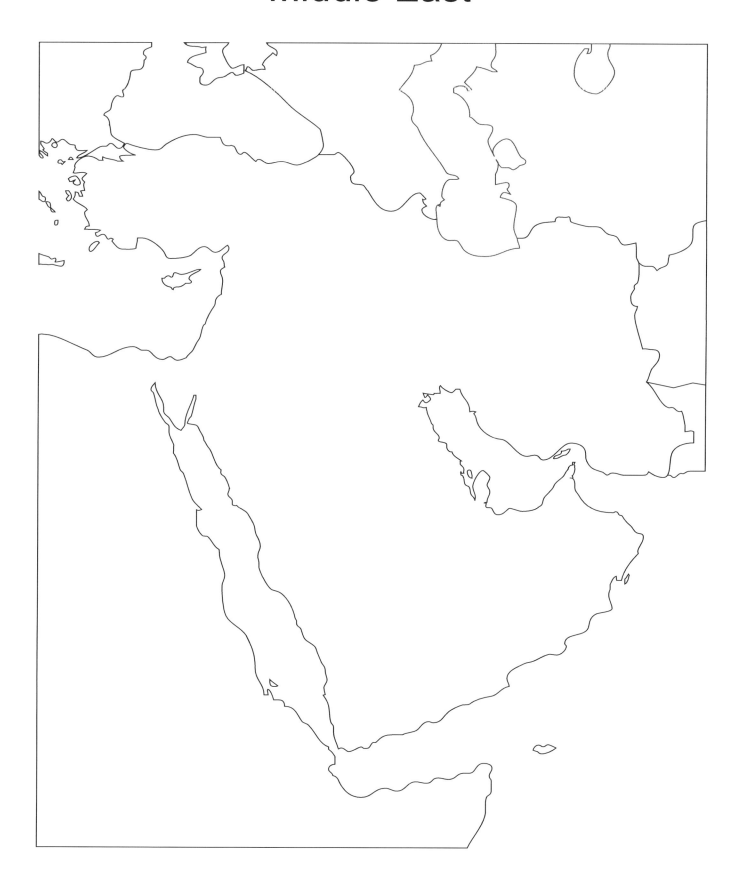

Middle East

GREECE

Crete

TURKEY

Adana

CYPRUS

Nicosia

Mediterranean Sea

SYRIA

IRAN

LEBANON

Beirut

Damascus

Baghdad

IRAQ

ISRAEL

Tel Aviv-Yafo

Jerusalem

Amman

STATE OF PALESTINE

West Bank

LIBYA

Alexandria

JORDAN

KUWAIT

Cairo

Kuwait

EGYPT

SAUDI ARABIA

Riyadh

Medina

Aswan

Red Sea

Jiddah

SUDAN

0   200 Kilometers

0   200 Nautical

Middle East

GREECE

Crete

TURKEY

CYPRUS

SYRIA

IRAN

LEBANON

IRAQ

ISRAEL

LIBYA

STATE OF PALESTINE

West Bank

JORDAN

KUWAIT

EGYPT

SAUDI ARABIA

SUDAN

0   200 Kilometers

0   200 Nautical

Middle East

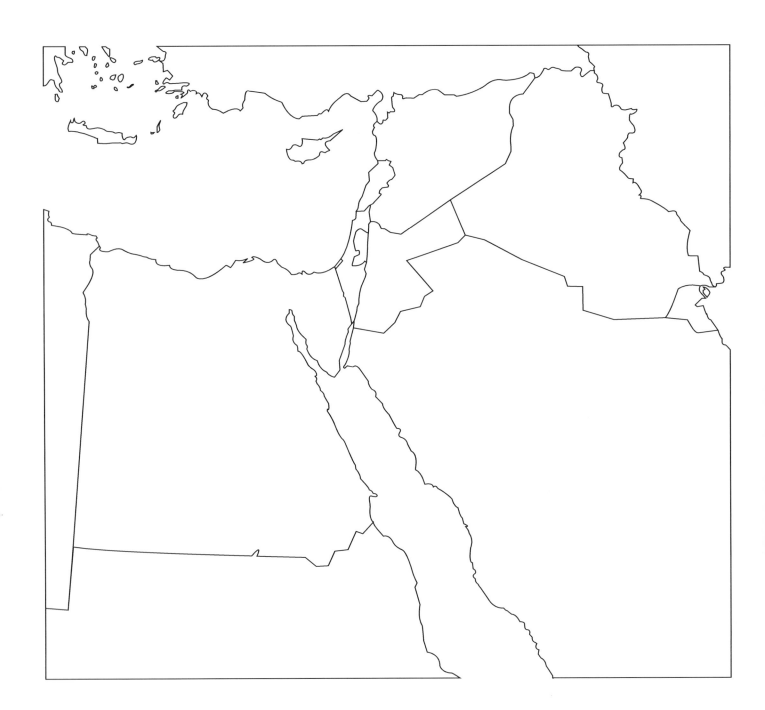

52

North America

Arctic Ocean

Ellesmere Island

GREENLAND (Denmark)

ICELAND

Barrow

Nome

Bearfort Sea

Baffin Bay

Banks Island

Baffin Island

Alaska (USA)

Anchorage

Victoria Island

Godthaab

Davis Strait

Great Bear Lake

Echo Bay

Iqaluit

Whitehorse

Labrador Sea

Juneau

Yellowknife

Great Slave Lake

Uranium City

Lake Athabasca

Hudson Bay

Goose Bay

St. John's

Prince Rupert

Churchill

Fort George

CANADA

Sydney

Edmonton

Lake Winnipeg

Quebec

St. John

Halifax

Vancouver

Calgary

Saskatoon

Regina

Winnipeg

Thunder Bay

Lake Superior

Montreal

Seattle

Lake Huron

Ottawa

Boston

North

Portland

Great Falls

Toronto

Lake Ontario

Detroit

Cleveland

New York

Philadelphia

North

Pacific

Boise

Minneapolis

Lake Michigan

Chicago

Lake Erie

Atlantic

Ocean

Salt Lake City

Omaha

Washington D.C.

Ocean

San Francisco

Denver

UNITED STATES

St. Louis

Louisville

Las Vegas

Los Angeles

Albuquerque

Little Rock

Atlanta

Charleston

San Diego

Phoenix

Dallas

Jacksonville

El Paso

New Orleans

Houston

Chihuahua

Miami

La Paz

MEXICO

Gulf of Mexico

CUBA

JAMAICA

Tampico

Mérida

Caribbean Sea

Guadalajara

Mexico

Veracruz

BELIZE

Acapulco

Oaxaca

HONDURAS

GUATEMALA

EL SALVADOR

North America

GREENLAND
(Denmark)

ICELAND

USA

CANADA

UNITED STATES

MEXICO

CUBA

JAMAICA

BELIZE

HONDURAS

GUATEMALA

EL SALVADOR

North America

55

North America

ALASKA

GREENLAND

ELLESMERE ISLAND

Beauton Sea

DEVON ISLAND

Baffin Bay

MELVILLE ISLAND

BANKS ISLAND

SOMERSET ISLAND

PRINCE OF WALES ISLAND

Davis Strait

VICTORIA ISLAND

YUKON

Great Bear Lake

NORTHWEST TERRITORY

NUNAVUT

PRINCE CHARLES ISLAND

BAFFIN ISLAND

Iqaluit ★

★ Whitehorse

Yellowknife ★

SOUTHHAMPTON ISLAND

Labrador Sea

Great Slave Lake

Hudson Bay

NEWFOUNDLAND AND LABRADOR

Juneau

Lake Athabasca

St. John's

BRITISH COLUMBIA

ALBERTA

SASKATCHEWAN

MANITOBA

James Bay

QUEBEC

Gulf of St. Lawrence

Pacific Ocean

Edmonton ★

Prince Edward Island

VANCOUVER ISLAND

Vancouver

Calgary

Saskatoon

Lake Winnipeg

ONTARIO

NEW BRUNSWICK

NOVA SCOTIA

Victoria ★

Regina ★

Lake Winnipegosis

Lake Nipigon

Quebec

Fredericton

Salt John

Halifax

Olympia

Winnipeg ★

MAINE

WASHINGTON

Thunder Bay

Lake Superior

Montreal

Augusta

Salem

Helena

NORTH DAKOTA

MINNESOTA

Ottawa

VERMONT

NEW HAMPSHIRE

Concord

Atlantic Ocean

OREGON

MONTANA

Bismark

Lake Huron

Toronto

Lake Ontario

NEW YORK

Albany

Boston

MASSACHUSETTS

Providence

RHODE ISLAND

Boise

SOUTH DAKOTA

Lake Michigan

MICHIGAN

Lansing

Lake Erie

Windsor

Hartford

CONNECTICUT

IDAHO

WYOMING

Pierre

Madison

WISCONSIN

PENNSYLVANIA

Harrisburg

Trenton

NEW JERSEY

NEVADA

Cheyenne

St. Paul

IOWA

Des Moines

NEBRASKA

Lincoln

ILLINOIS

Springfield

INDIANA

Indianapolis

OHIO

Columbus

Dover

DELAWARE

Washington D.C.

MARYLAND

Sacramento

Carson City

Salt Lake City

Denver

Jefferson City

Frankfort

WEST VIRGINIA

Charleston

Richmond

VIRGINIA

UTAH

COLORADO

KANSAS

Topeka

MISSOURI

KENTUCKY

Raleigh

NORTH CAROLINA

CALIFORNIA

Santa Fe

Nashville

TENNESSEE

Columbia

Phoenix

ARIZONA

NEW MEXICO

OKLAHOMA

Oklahoma City

ARKANSAS

Little Rock

MISSISSIPPI

Atlanta

SOUTH CAROLINA

Jackson

Montgomery

GEORGIA

TEXAS

ALABAMA

Tallahassee

Austin

Baton Rouge

LOUISIANA

Atlantic Ocean

Honolulu

HAWAII

BAJA CALIFORNIA NORTE

SONORA

CHIHUAHUA

Chihuahua

Gulf of Mexico

FLORDIA

Nassau

THE BAHAMAS

COAHUILA

BAJA CALIFORNIA SUR

SINALOA

DURANGO

NUEVO LEON

Havana

CUBA

DOMINICAN REPUBLIC

La Paz

ZACATECAS

TAMAULIPAS

San Juan

SAN LUIS POTOSI

Tampico

MEXICO

George Town

CAYMAN ISLANDS

HAITI

Santo Domingo

PUERTO RICO

Pacific Ocean

NAYARIT

AGUASCALIENTES

GUANAJUATO

QUERETARO

HIDALGO

VERACRUZ

Veracruz

YUCATAN

QUINTANA ROO

Port-au-Prince

JAMAICA

Kingston

Guadalajara

JALISCO

MEXICO

Mexico City

MORELOS

PUEBLA

CAMPECHE

BELIZE

COLIMA

MICHOACAN

DISTRITO FEDERAL

Oaxaca

Belmopan

GUERRERO

CHIAPAS

Caribbean Sea

Acapulco

OAXACA

GUATEMALA

HONDURAS

ARUBA

Guatemala

Tegucigalpa

San Salvador

NICARAGUA

EL SALVADOR

Managua

COSTA RICA

San José

PANAMA

Panama

VENEZUELA

COLOMBIA

56

North America

ALASKA

GREENLAND

ELLESMERE ISLAND

DEVON ISLAND

BANKS ISLAND

MELVILLE ISLAND

SOMERSET ISLAND

PRINCE OF WALES ISLAND

VICTORIA ISLAND

YUKON

NORTHWEST TERRITORY

NUNAVUT

BAFFIN ISLAND

PRINCE CHARLES ISLAND

SOUTHHAMPTON ISLAND

Juneau

NEWFOUNDLAND AND LABRADOR

BRITISH COLUMBIA

ALBERTA

MANITOBA

QUEBEC

VANCOUVER ISLAND

ONTARIO

Prince Edward Island

SASKATCHEWAN

NEW BRUNSWICK

NOVA SCOTIA

MAINE

WASHINGTON

MONTANA

NORTH DAKOTA

MINNESOTA

VERMONT

NEW HAMPSHIRE

OREGON

SOUTH DAKOTA

WISCONSIN

MICHIGAN

NEW YORK

MASSACHUSETTS

RHODE ISLAND

CONNECTICUT

IDAHO

WYOMING

IOWA

PENNSYLVANIA

NEW JERSEY

NEVADA

NEBRASKA

INDIANA

OHIO

DELAWARE

MARYLAND

ILLINOIS

UTAH

COLORADO

KANSAS

MISSOURI

KENTUCKY

WEST VIRGINIA

VIRGINIA

CALIFORNIA

NORTH CAROLINA

ARIZONA

OKLAHOMA

ARKANSAS

TENNESSEE

SOUTH CAROLINA

NEW MEXICO

MISSISSIPPI

ALABAMA

GEORGIA

HAWAII

TEXAS

LOUISIANA

FLORDIA

BAJA CALIFORNIA NORTE

SONORA

CHIHUAHUA

THE BAHAMAS

BAJA CALIFORNIA SUR

COAHUILA

SINALOA

NUEVO LEON

CUBA

DOMINICAN REPUBLIC

DURANGO

ZACATECAS

SAN LUIS POTOSI

TAMAULIPAS

CAYMAN ISLANDS

HAITI

PUERTO RICO

NAYARIT

AGUASCALIENTES

MEXICO

GUANAJUATO

VERACRUZ

YUCATAN

JAMAICA

QUERETARO

HIDALGO

JALISCO

DISTRITO FEDERAL

TLAXCALA

MEXICO

QUINTANA ROO

COLIMA

MICHOACAN

MORELOS

PUEBLA

BAHIA DE CAMPECHE

CAMPECHE

GUERRERO

BELIZE

ARUBA

OAXACA

CHIAPAS

GUATEMALA

HONDURAS

VENEZUELA

EL SALVADOR

NICARAGUA

COLOMBIA

COSTA RICA

PANAMA

North America

Juneau

North America

South America

North Atlantic Ocean

South Pacific Ocean

South Atlantic Ocean

Barranquilla

Panama
PANAMA

Medellin

Cali

Bogota

COLOMBIA

Quito
ECUADOR
Guayaquil

Piura

Iquitos

Caracas

Valenci a

San Cristobal

VENEZUELA

Port-of-Spain
TRINIDAD AND TABAGO

Georgetown

GUYANA

Paramaribo

SURINAME

Cayenne

FRENCH GUIANA

Macapa

Santarem

PERU

Lima

Cusco

Rio Branco

Porto Velho

BRAZIL

Teresina

Fortaleza

Natal

Maceio

Salvador

Trinidad

La Paz
BOLIVIA

Santa Cruz

Cuiaba

Brasilia

Goiania

Uberlandia

Arica

Iquique

Potosi

Campo Grande

PARAGUAY

Asuncion

Vitoria

Rio de Janeiro

Curitiba

Florianopolis

CHILE

Salta

Resistencia

Cordoba

Santa Fe

Mendoza

Santiago

Buenos Aires
La Plata

Porto Alegre

Salto
URUGUAY
Montevideo

ARGENTINA

Mar del Plata

Puerto Montt

San Carlos de Bariloche

Comodoro Rivadavia

Rio Gallego

Strait of Magellan

Stanley
Falkland Islands

South Georgia and the South Sandwich Islands

Ushuaia

0   500 Kilometers
0   500 Miles

South America

PANAMA

TRINIDAD AND TABAGO

North Atlantic Ocean

VENEZUELA

COLOMBIA

GUYANA

SURINAME

FRENCH GUIANA

ECUADOR

PERU

BRAZIL

BOLIVIA

PARAGUAY

CHILE

ARGENTINA

URUGUAY

0   500 Kilometers

0   500 Miles

Falkland Islands

South Georgia and the
South Sandwich Islands

South America

South America

63

Latin America

UNITED STATES

Los Angeles

El Paso

New Orleans

BERMUDA

North

Atlantic

Ocean

Monterrey

Gulf of Mexico

Miami

Nassau

MEXICO

Havana

THE BAHAMAS

Guadalajara

CUBA

DOMINICAN REPUBLIC

Mexico

JAMAICA

HAITI

Santo Domingo

BELIZE

Kingston

Port-au-Prince

PUERTO RICO

Belmopan

DOMINICA

Guatemala

HONDURAS

ST. LUCIA

North

GUATEMALA

Caribbean Sea

BARBADOS

San Salvador

Tegucigalpa

TRINIDAD AND TOBAGO

Pacific

EL SALVADOR

NICARAGUA

Port-of-Spain

Managua

San José

GUYANA

Ocean

COSTA

Panama

Caracas

RICA

VENEZUELA

Georgetown

PANAMA

Paramaribo

FRENCH GUIANA

Medellin

Cayenne

Bogotá

SURINAME

COLOMBIA

Cali

GALAPAGOS ISLANDS

ECUADOR

Quito

Belém

Manaus

Fortaleza

Trujillo

PERU

BRAZIL

Salvador

Lima

La Paz

South

BOLIVIA

Brasilia

Pacific

Ocean

PARAGUAY

Sao Paulo

Antofagasta

Asunción

Rio de Janeiro

CHILE

Rosario

Santiago

Buenos Aires

URUGUAY

Concepción

Montevideo

South

ARGENTINA

Atlantic

Ocean

0   1000 Miles

FALKLAND ISLANDS

Cape Horn

64

Latin America

UNITED STATES

BERMUDA

MEXICO

THE BAHAMAS

CUBA

DOMINICAN REPUBLIC

JAMAICA   HAITI

BELIZE   PUERTO RICO

HONDURAS

GUATEMALA   DOMINICA

ST. LUCIA

EL SALVADOR   NICARAGUA   BARBADOS

TRINIDAD AND TOBAGO

COSTA
RICA   VENEZUELA   GUYANA

PANAMA   SURINAME

FRENCH GUIANA

COLOMBIA

ECUADOR

GALAPAGOS ISLANDS

PERU   BRAZIL

BOLIVIA

PARAGUAY

CHILE

ARGENTINA

URUGUAY

FALKLAND ISLANDS

0   1000 Miles

65

Latin America

Southeast Asia

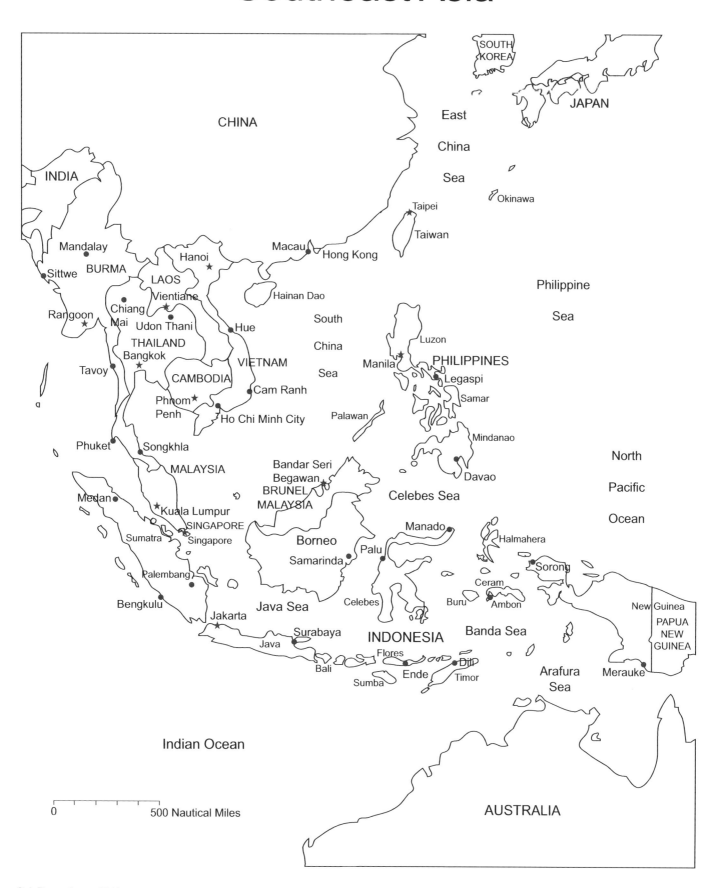

CHINA

INDIA

SOUTH KOREA

JAPAN

East China Sea

Okinawa

Mandalay

Hanoi

Sittwe

BURMA

LAOS

Macau

Hong Kong

Taipei

Taiwan

Rangoon

Chiang Mai

Vientiane

Hainan Dao

Philippine Sea

Udon Thani

Hue

South China Sea

Luzon

THAILAND

Bangkok

VIETNAM

Manila

PHILIPPINES

Legaspi

Tavoy

CAMBODIA

Phnom Penh

Cam Ranh

Samar

Ho Chi Minh City

Palawan

Mindanao

Phuket

Songkhla

Davao

MALAYSIA

Bandar Seri Begawan

BRUNEI

Celebes Sea

North Pacific Ocean

Medan

Kuala Lumpur

MALAYSIA

Manado

Halmahera

SINGAPORE

Singapore

Borneo

Palu

Sorong

Sumatra

Samarinda

Celebes

Ceram

Buru

Ambon

New Guinea

Palembang

Java Sea

Banda Sea

PAPUA NEW GUINEA

Bengkulu

Jakarta

INDONESIA

Surabaya

Arafura Sea

Merauke

Java

Flores

Dili

Bali

Ende

Timor

Sumba

Indian Ocean

AUSTRALIA

0   500 Nautical Miles

Southeast Asia

CHINA

SOUTH
KOREA

JAPAN

Okinawa

INDIA

Taiwan

Macau
Hong Kong

BURMA

LAOS

THAILAND

PHILIPPINES

CAMBODIA

VIETNAM

MALAYSIA

BRUNEI

MALAYSIA

SINGAPORE

Borneo

INDONESIA

PAPUA
NEW
GUINEA

0   500 Nautical Miles

AUSTRALIA

Southeast Asia

Eastern Europe

ce Jones 2011
uce jonespublishing.com

Eastern Europe

SWEDEN

ESTONIA

RUSSIA

DENMARK

LATVIA

LITHUANIA

RUSSIA

NETHERLANDS

BELARUS

BELGIUM

POLAND

GERMANY

LUX

CZECH REPUBLIC

UKRAINE

FRANCE

SLOVAKIA

LIECH.

AUSTRIA

SWITZERLAND

HUNGARY

MOLDOVA

SLOVENIA

ROMANIA

MONACO

CROATIA

BOSNIA AND HERZEGOVINA

Corsica

ITALY

SERBIA

BULGARIA

MONTENEGRO

KOSOVO

Sardinia

F.Y.R.O.M.

ALBANIA

GREECE

TURKEY

Ionian Sea

ALGERIA

Sicily

Rhodes

TUNISIA

MALTA

Crete

0   300 Kilometers

0   300 Miles

Eastern Europe

Eastern Europe – Baltic Region

GERMANY
CZECH REPUBLIC
POLAND
SLOVAK REPUBLIC
UKRAINE
• Munich
Vienna ★   ★ Bratislava
AUSTRIA
★ Budapest
• Innsbruck
HUNGARY
Ljubljana
ROMANIA
★
SLOVENIA
Venice •
★ Zagreb
CROATIA
BOSNIA -
HERZEGOVINA
Belgrade ★
ITALY
Split
Adriatic
Sea
Sarajevo ★
SERBIA
•
MONTENEGRO
Pristina
Sofia
Dubrovnik
★
★
★ Rome
Podgorica
KOSOVO
BULGARIA
★
Skopje
Naples •
Tirane
★
MACEDONIA
Tyrrhenian
Sea
ALBANIA
Aegean
Sea
GREECE
Palermo
•
Ionian
Sea
Sicily
Athens
★

0   100   200 Kilometers

0   100   200 Nautical Miles

Eastern Europe – Baltic Region

GERMANY
CZECH REPUBLIC
POLAND
SLOVAK REPUBLIC
UKRAINE
AUSTRIA
HUNGARY
SLOVENIA
ROMANIA
CROATIA
BOSNIA - HERZEGOVINA
SERBIA
ITALY
MONTENEGRO
KOSOVO
BULGARIA
MACEDONIA
ALBANIA
GREECE
Sicily

0   100   200 Kilometers

0   100   200 Nautical Miles

Eastern Europe – Baltic Region

Scandinavia

Barents Sea

Murmansk

White Sea

FINLAND

Lake Ladoga

SWEDEN

Gulf of Bothnia

Helsinki

Gulf of Finland   St. Petersburg

NORWAY

Oslo

Stockholm

ALAND ISLANDS

Tallinn

ESTONIA

RUSSIA

Moscow

Stavanger

Goteborg

Gotland

Baltic Sea

Oland

Riga   LATVIA

North Sea

DENMARK

LITHUANIA

Vilnius

Copenhagen

Bornholm

Kaliningrad   RUSSIA

Minsk

Gdansk

BELARUS

Hamburg

NETHERLANDS

Bremen   Berlin

Warsaw

Brest

Amsterdam

GERMANY

POLAND

UKRAINE   Kiev

0   300 Kilometers

0   300 Miles

Scandinavia

0   300 Kilometers
0   300 Miles

NORWAY

SWEDEN

FINLAND

Lake Ladoga

RUSSIA

ALAND ISLANDS

ESTONIA

Gotland

LATVIA

DENMARK

Oland

LITHUANIA

RUSSIA

Bornholm

BELARUS

NETHERLANDS

GERMANY

POLAND

UKRAINE

Scandinavia

Mediterranean Sea Region

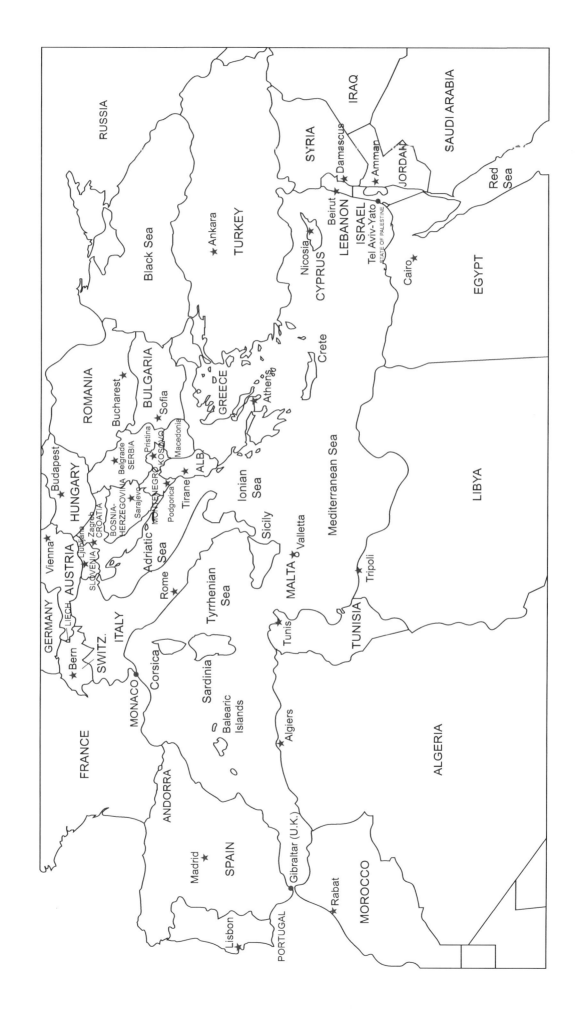

79

Mediterranean Sea Region

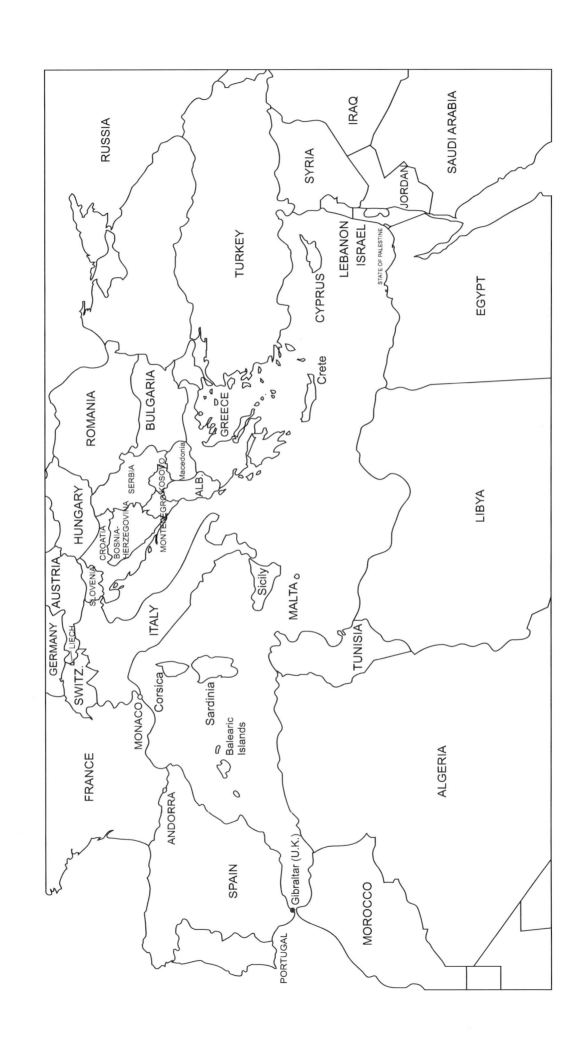

Mediterranean Sea Region

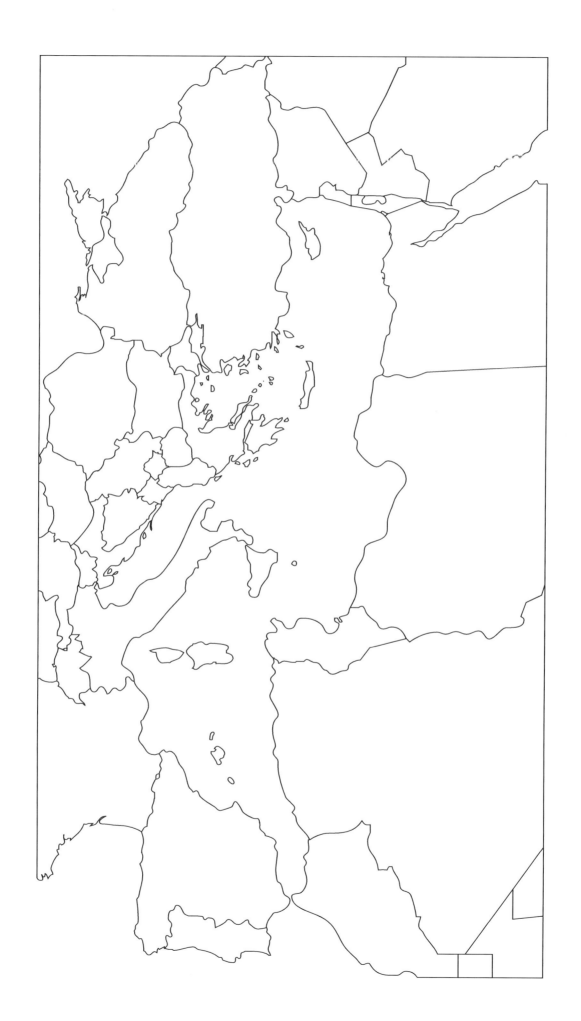

United States of America

United States of America

United States of America

Canada

ELLESMERE
ISLAND

DEVON
ISLAND

Baffin
Bay

Beauton
Sea

BANKS
ISLAND

MELVILLE
ISLAND

SOMERSET
ISLAND

PRINCE OF
WALES
ISLAND

VICTORIA
ISLAND

BAFFIN
ISLAND

Davis
Strait

YUKON

Whitehorse

Great Bear
Lake

NORTHWEST
TERRITORY

Yellowknife

Great Slave
Lake

NUNAVUT

PRINCE
CHARLES
ISLAND

Iqaluit

SOUTHHAMPTON
ISLAND

Labrador
Sea

Lake
Athabasca

Hudson
Bay

NEWFOUNDLAND and LABRADOR

St. John's

BRITISH
COLUMBIA

ALBERTA

SASKATCHEWAN

MANITOBA

James
Bay

QUEBEC

Gulf of
St. Lawrence

VANCOUVER
ISLAND

Edmonton

Saskatoon

Lake
Winnipeg

ONTARIO

Prince Edward
Island

NEW
BRUNSWICK

NOVA
SCOTIA

Vancouver

Calgary

Regina

Lake
Winnipegosis

Lake
Nipigon

Fredericton

Victoria

Winnipeg

Quebec

Saint John

Halifax

Thunder Bay

Lake
Superior

Montreal

Ottawa

Lake
Huron

Toronto

Lake
Ontario

Windsor

Lake
Erie

Lake
Michigan

Canada

Canada

Made in the USA
Lexington, KY
21 January 2014